I Reckon is an honest, poignant look at the Past, from within the medium of poetry. From Alexander's experimental "forbidden haibun," where the prose sections are supported with haiku-like verse, to his unapologetic and insightful haiku, this book tells the story of growing up in Sandusky, Ohio, and other interesting locales. Childhood memories are interspersed with character studies and descriptive scenes of nature in an elegant style that is at once tender and blatant. Francis Alexander captures the Zen feel of peaceful calm while evoking all manner of emotions from the Reader. This book is already a favorite of mine—and will be one of yours as well.

~t.santitoro, editor, *Scifaikuest* poetry magazine

Other Books by Francis W. Alexander

While Treating My Lady at Zom's Rib Shack, the Waiter Inquired How I Escaped the Pot (Panic Press)

When the Mushrooms Come (Alban Lake, 2019).

I Reckon

Haiku & Haibun

Francis Wesley Alexander

Paul Laurence Dunbar Series

Bottom Dog Press

Huron, OH

Credits

General Editor: Larry Smith
Cover design: Susanna Sharp Schwacke
Cover art: Richard Sherman
Author photo by Jamaal Brewer
Photos provided by the author

Acknowledgments

I wish to acknowledge the many publications that have published my poems. A few haibun such as "The Pre Home-Going Party," have been slightly changed. Some of the haibun have been published in both *Contemporary Haibun Online* and *Contemporary Haibun* (hard copy). I also acknowledge *Failed Haiku, Volume 2, Issue 20,* 2017; *Full of Moonlight: Haiku Society of America 2016 Members' Anthology*, and the *Haiku Handbook: How to Write, Share, and Teach Haiku* as well as those publications in the notes at the end of the book.

I also wish to thank Larry Smith of Bottom Dog Press for his support of this book. Thanks to Lyn Reese, Ray Rasmussen, Adelaide B. Shaw, and the other members of my former Haibun Writers' Group for their critiques of my work. I am also thankful to Lenard D Moore, the late Robert Spiess and Henry Lewis Sanders for their wisdom and publishing of many of my haiku.

For Mack Gilmer, (my stepfather)
Jim Irby, (my uncle)
Teresa Irby and Sharon Irby Brewer, (my cousins)

Contents

Author's Note

This is a record of my life, told in the form of haiku, haibun, senryu, and other short poems.

A haiku is a poem consisting of seventeen syllables or less. The haiku poet always includes at least one of the five senses of sight, sound, smell, taste, and touch in the poem. A "season word", that is, anything that describes winter, spring, summer, and fall is also included in most haiku. When one reads a haiku, the poem should place the reader in his or her own experience. For example, when I write a haiku of my beach moment, the reader should be taken to his or her own beach experience. Following is an example of my haiku that was published in the *Haiku Society of America's 2016 Members' Anthology*.

> spring feeding
> the small black bird's joy
> is my moment

A senryu is also a seventeen-syllable poem minus the season words. This kind of poem is usually humorous in nature. In the following senryu, which was published in *Failed Haiku*, I was tired before seeing the kittens. I was entertained by them and no longer tired.

> morning fatigue—
> the transferred energy
> of kittens at play

A haibun, according to Williamson and Harter in their Haiku Handbook, is a short essay in prose with "haiku mixed in." Basho, a Japanese poet, was known for his haibun. Basho's travel journals feature a lot of his haibun. This book is meant to be a travel journal as I continue down life's path. In *I Reckon*, I give the sights, sounds, tastes, and other sensations of my times on the Southside of Sandusky, at Cedar Point Amusement Park; throughout Ohio, Michigan, and Detroit.

I gave this book the title "I Reckon" in honor of Mrs. Effie McNair, affectionately known as "Granny," who impressed me greatly whenever I went to visit her grandson Cliff. Her cupcakes were pleasant to the sight, nose, and taste buds. As in other neighborhoods, the Southside of Sandusky was a village and Granny was one of the villagers who helped raised me.

I Reckon

This cloudless night, I gaze at the moon and stars, and wonder how many worlds out there harbor life? If they are anything like us, do they war and have religion. Hopefully, the more advanced have gotten past the primitive violence that we have here. I wonder if they too have their Beyonce and Jessie J. Are there homeless beings who live amongst other beings who have plenty, or does everyone have his own piece of land where he can farm and provide for himself, and contribute to his society without stress? Do they have nations? Do these nations compete against each other in sport instead of war? Do they ride golden horned unicorns and scoff that horses are things of fantasy? Most of all, I wonder if there is a two-legged being living on a street in a community he is proud of, in a city that provides him lifetime memories of a marvelous state, within a wonderful country, on a vast continent, that is a subset of the nations on his earth, surrounded by other planets.
I reckon there is.

brutally cold night

the stars far too distant

for homeless warmth

Childhood on the Southside of Sandusky, Ohio

Forbidden Haibun: A School Day

Blue skies: we trudge the few blocks to the neighborhood school. Perfume scent: after the bell rings, the announcements come. Warm breeze: pin drop silence when the teacher leaves. Nest of hungry birds: the refreshing feeling of unbridled freedom. That click clack sound: running back to our seats before the teacher enters.

crackle

of the public address system

howling wind

Flash card game: before I see the numbers, my foe answers. Torrid afternoon: squirming in my seat as I take the test. Sudden sunshine: grinning that my school project was accepted.

Christmas play

the teacher picks me

for a minor part

Recess: I try to be the first in line. Warm breeze: that elated feeling of releasing a shout. End of break: looking to see who's last in line. Swirling leaves: too busy having fun to look at the clock. School bell rings: the sound of teachers shouting and the scurry of feet.

autumn leaves

as cliques move down the sidewalks

that girl teases me

Uncle Bishe: A Haibun

If you're a Baby Boomer, you can probably remember
the old lady and her kind and tender habits as she
waited on you from behind the counter of your favorite
Mom and Pop store. It was a given that the lady who
waited on you was a tender soul, not far from an angel
like Miss Lonae Mae who, it is rumored, once coached
a boys' baseball team in Sandusky. But how many can
remember the very mean man, the one with the scowl
so hot several fire department hoses couldn't extinguish
it. As you stood quivering, and peeking up at the horror
facing you, you yearned to get away. You twisted and
turned, fighting to keep the yellow results of your fear
from leaving your body because they didn't have
Depends back then and peer pressure was nothing to
laugh at since that kind of bad reputation lasted forever
when you were young.

humid night

that pest of a gnat

just won't go away

A bad Clint Eastwood character was Mother Theresa
compared to the terror facing you. "Whaddya want!
Hurry up, four eyes!" It was hard to think with his boda-
cious blistering banter. You'd forgotten the name of the
candy bar you had a strong hankering for. Wouldn't it
have been better if he could pick out what you needed?
"Okay, little tyke," he could say as he patted you on the
head, "you want bologna, milk, ketchup, and a Hershey
bar." But no, even if he did have knowledge of your
needs, he'd still have something nasty to say. The split
second you opened your mouth, he'd roar, "Hurry up! I
don't have all day." And although you were due a two
cent deposit on your returned Pepsi bottle, he'd count it
as one cent and say, "This ain't enough," as he counted
the coins on his palm and you dug around in your pock-
ets for the coin that would get you out of your misery.

These days, I bump into someone from the hood who remembers, because they faced that fear too. Then, it was a horror movie. Now, it's comedy. It is the kind of laughter therapists say aids good health. You feel good splitting your guts at someone else's haiku moment which is now your story.

Fall breezes

the new kitten hopping

alongside its mother

Good Hands: A Haibun

His name was Cliff and he lived in a white house on Filmore Street. They say the dark-skinned string bean was a turn-the-other-cheek Christian. To me, he was just nice and quiet. But some kids, like Lawrence, my own brash burly bully, didn't tolerate that kind of behavior. Lawrence walked right up and did the traditional shove-the-weakling-in-order-to-bully-him routine. That was a mistake.

The next day, the rumor of Cliff defeating Lawrence in a fist fight spread like pollen. It taught me to beware of vexing "the quiet ones." No one else bothered the kid with the "good hands." The fight did not change him. Cliff stayed humble and quiet. When he died of cancer before graduating from grade school, I was confident he was in God's good hands.

breakfast

the kitten's tender grasp

of my finger

The Stickleback: A Haibun

Shortly before bedtime, Grandma shows me a letter
and newspaper article she received from Uncle Billy, a
submariner. In the article is a picture of the submarine
USS Stickleback lying on its side after a collision with
the destroyer *Silverstein*.

I read part of Uncle Billy's letter aloud, "Our sub had
lost power and we were sinking to dangerous depths.
We worked frantically to get the ship to surface. We
succeeded in surfacing only to be accidentally rammed
by the *Silverstein*. To keep the *Stickleback* afloat, the
Silverstein remained stuck into our sub. Miraculously,
no lives were lost. The diamond earrings I bought for
you in Tahiti were destroyed."

Bath time—

dipping the toy submarine

under the suds

A Parent's Workday: A Haibun

To my horror the tamper stops on the bridge spanning
Sandusky Bay. The gale howls and smacks me from
three sides no matter where I position myself. Watching
Grandpap and the railroad men work on the rails, I rub
my chill pinched fingers, keep a look out for trains, and
complain. I want the impossible—to go home.

frozen lake

a bird takes flight

for the clouds

After leaving the bridge we head for one destination
near my street. My spirits are raised when Grandpap
lets me get off the tamper and head home. I trudge on
aching toes across the rails and through the wood to-
wards my neighborhood and home.

coal burning stove—

the toy train derailing

near the bridge

Haiku Moments in My Hometown

frigid day
meat loaf scent wafting
from the oven

Football Friday night
an orange oblong moon
on the field's puddle

spring shower
dark hands skinning catfish
in the kitchen sink

scorching heat
I flinch
at your touch

that much welcome tune
of the ice cream truck
dog days

receding thunderstorm
on top of the siren's wail
the train's whistle

badminton
with each chirp from the front
a backyard response

Summer evening
the dragonfly skirts
the full checker board

Summer evening
the gnats form a sphere
hovering and waiting

Hot summer nights
the Motown sound
dancing in the streets

Forbidden Haibun: Summer School Camp

Summer breeze: Ms. Peters unlocks the huge games box.
On the blacktop, we play many games. Swift breeze:
I see why Lynn places first in Junior Olympics. Dodge
ball: they all seem to be taking aim at me. Baseball
diamond: needing one more player, they call for me.
Blue skies: playing red rover on the black top. Lone
daisy: watching the girls play hopscotch. Blaring sun:
Ray Hulin shouts, "Babe Ruth," and points his bat.

hot

near the baseball diamond

a postman parks

Hours from sunset, Ms. Peters closes the box and leaves
us to play. Sun's glare: heads shaved, both Ray and
"Boot" fight on the playground. Distant clouds: legends
that Uncle Jim knocked a softball over the school.

smell of earthworms—

all the playground art

is washed away

Moments of Hobo Junction
and Other Childhood Haunts

Summer afternoon
the dragonfly skims
along the railroad tracks

                              from the tracks
                              down the hill
                              Hobo Junction–ferns

behind the dragonfly
balancing on brook crossed logs
young explorers

summer morn
floating on the brown viscous pond
rocks draped green

Monarch butterfly
just over that hill
the railroad tracks

                                    the sun's glare—
                                    with nothing to discover
                                    we head for home

Icons: A Haibun

As a kid, I was enthralled by well-known sports stars and other celebrities. Wide-eyed, I often heard rumors that people I knew were related to famous people. I remember hearing that my seventh-grade classmate Yance Pepitone was related to New York Yankees baseball player, Joe Pepitone; and John Mayfield was kin to Curtis Mayfield of the singing group, The Impressions. James Thom, my middle school homeroom teacher, had a brother named Leonard who saved future President John F Kennedy's life when the PT 109 sank.

blue skies

I'm jealous that his kite

flies so high

Situated between Cleveland and Toledo and not far from Detroit, it wasn't hard to imagine that I could be related to a notable person, be they national or local. I was pleased to learn that my grandfather, Lloyd Alexander, was said to have beaten the world's checker champion. I was pretty good myself and saw how masterful he was whenever I played against him.

fragrant breeze—

she mows patterns

across the lawn

I was proud of my uncle Bill because he worked as an engineer at NASA. My senior year we students went to the facility and I remember being slightly disappointed at not being able to see him. He owned a white T-bird with red upholstery and was notorious for installing 45 record players in cars around Sandusky. At that time, there were no CDs, eight-track tapes, or cassette tapes. When our family went on long car trips, we found it hard to find AM radio stations that played music I liked. There was no FM at the time.

Indians vs Yankees
the organ music plays
between innings

Urban Legends: A Haibun

It was the year of my high school graduation. Pitch black ruled the breezy May evening. The car's high beams formed a shell that pushed away the gloom. As our car hobbled down that Sandusky County dirt road, I straightened the collar around my neck to protect it from the sudden chill. Was the Elmore Ghost Rider really going to spring out of the rows of corn stalks? I was also apprehensive because I couldn't wait to be in her audience at the after party.

Earlier that evening, I sat in the chair in the dressing room. I felt like the luckiest man in the world as Nancy did my makeup in preparation for my bit part in the play *Arsenic and Old Lace*. For some reason, I was depressed. She convinced me to ride with some of the crew in search of the headless motorcyclist. She was riding with her boyfriend to the site and would join us at the party afterwards.

snap of potato chips

a bug's body splatters

on the windshield

Legend had it that the motorcyclist had run into a barbed wire fence and was decapitated. Now, on spring nights, he can be seen riding the countryside like Irving's headless horseman in search of his head. Seeing neither specter nor her group, we headed back to Sandusky. As I sat in the party room amongst fellow guests, my apprehension grew thicker by the second. Where was this angel? The jokes told and games played were dusts in the wind. An hour after the party started, the host's mother walked into the room and told us that there had been an automobile accident.

silence—

the rows of Styrofoam cups

left unused

Practice Makes Perfect: A Haibun

I remember that spring day when David "Bo" Rather broke the high school pole vault record. With the sun beaming high above and a tender breeze tickling my face, I watched Bo hold the pole at an angle. With a spring in his step, he sprinted towards the pole vault pit. The click-clack sound of his cleats hitting the black asphalt intensified as he moved. Gliding as gracefully as an eagle, he sailed over the bar, setting the record.

I think further back to my grade school days when I went to that abandoned factory on Filmore Street. One day, after visiting Aunt Rita and Uncle George, I walked across the street to an abandoned factory. As the sun smiled down on me, I watched Bo and Monte Crabb set up a makeshift pole vault pit. I was puzzled by them performing this action since black males usually excelled at running, the long jump, the shot put, and long-distance events. Never would I have imagined their actions paying future dividends for them.

It paid big dividends. Bo excelled as one of the top pole vaulters in the State of Ohio. Two years later, Monte became one of the state's best vaulters. He broke Bo's high school record which still stands forty-eight years later.

lilac scent

an ant finding another route

to pull the beetle

Cedar Point

Blue Light Haibun

As the wind howls and blows outside my window, I sit at my computer cleaning out the email inbox. "Blue light posters," the Spencer's advertisement proclaims. Memories surface of my time working in Hotel Breakers' Coffee Shop Restaurant where I washed dishes for the Anchor Room next door.

My friends Peck, Sam, and Willie P wore black pants, white shirts with red bow ties. They carried the huge oval trays to the dishwashing counter. I remember the many-colored plastic toothpicks in the shape of swords and lobster and other special foods that we had to scrape off the dishes. We poured various sorts of wine and mixed drinks down the drain. I remember the time Peck showed me the five dollars that jazz trombonist Al Hirt gave him for a tip.

The Anchor room was a mysterious place that might as well be as far away as China since dishwashers were usually forbidden entrance. There were always exceptions. Once I was permitted to enter that hallowed place to deliver silverware. Candlelight competed with blue light and belly danced off the love-entranced faces of finely dressed couples. On the wall, a huge mural of a ship at anchor bathed in blue bobbed below the moon's yellow grin. I wanted to hop into the picture, bask in its blue glow as the water licked my face, and just listen to the soothing roar and swash of the waves.

doughnut breakfast—

the powdered grey cheeks

of the morning sky

The Trip: A Haibun

The last ferry departed two hours ago. Thick clouds obstruct the moonlight while those farther west blink like fireflies. Peck and I stand at the slip, observe the waves whipping our supervisor Dave's speedboat. Had I known the weather would be like this, I would have told Peck that he'd have to stay and clean up the Coffee Shop by himself.

humid night
counting the moments
between thunderclaps

Dave pulls the cord to his outboard motor, and we're off. Besides his attempts to console us, the only sounds are the slapping of the waves as the boat plows over each crest, the motor's hum, and the distant thunder. We hug and clasp the rocking boat, two teenagers laughing at each dip as if we're on one of the park's roller coasters. A quarter of the way to our destination, Peck says, "Suppose the motor conks out."

dark marina
the ferry rocking
from side to side

Approach: A Haibun

Full moon. Exhausted after a long workday at the Coffee Shop, the three of us plod towards the parking lot. As we move to the right of the Hotel Breakers front entrance, six men in black leather jackets form an arc around us. I think about the rumors of Hells Angels storming Cedar Point Amusement Park, but nothing has happened yet. We slow down, the half circle constricts, we stop. One giant of a man with hair flowing down his back and looking like a fanged Viking approaches and asks in a raspy voice, "Where's the party around here?"

cotton candy smell

a lone seagull strutting down

the moonlit causeway

Shocks: A Haibun

I took the amusement park job to keep from being home-less. The corporation let its workers stay in one of the dorms for less than fifteen dollars a week, which suited me fine. When I first came to the men's dorms, it didn't trouble me that women walked the halls as frequently as ghosts in a haunted motel. What struck me was the men's restroom. It had no locks, especially the one next to my room. Nor was there a sign that said "mens" or "ladies." I wanted to avoid the embarrassment of walking into what could actually be the ladies' room, so I investigated each piece of the bathroom entrance like Columbo and found nothing but a sign that said, "No cameras allowed."

Then it happened one morning. Brushing my teeth at the bathroom sink I blinked and squinted my eyes to make sure I was seeing correctly. A young Polish female had entered and proceeded to do her business at the sink next to me.

It took days for the shock to wear off. By that time, I had searched for and found a slightly larger bathroom sever-al doors down. I was determined not to be surprised in a different way. I surmised that the bathroom next to me had been the ladies' room, so I'd use the newly discovered one. I was wrong in my assumptions. A week or so later as I'd finished doing my business a Russian female en-tered. "Sorry," she said as her Rs formed into Ls and then walked to the sink to prepare herself for work. Nothing surprises me anymore.

Midwestern summer—

beneath tornado clouds

a siren wails

The roar of the waves greet my ears as I open the door
and step into the hall. A cool September breeze makes
its morning jog down the awakening hallway. Sever-
al doors down an occupant is sitting outside his door,
talking on the phone. I still feel odd not hearing the
crinkle and clank of the roller coaster although the park
won't open for another hour. With a twist to the right I
lock the door and step to the restroom next to me. Who
knows what surprises await?

I push the tavern-like door. When I enter, the open
window, with many small dead insects littering its sill,
greets me. I wash my hands, dry them, and turn to
leave when I look up. I wonder how I missed the mon-
strosity upon entering. It's as if I've just been placed as
a character in a grade B horror flick. I've never seen one
that big.

perched upside down
on the bathroom's ceiling
a dragonfly

Fantastic: A Haibun

Tonight at 11:30 Cedar Point is showing the movie *Fantastic Four* and giving away their award winning four-dollar fries to employees in appreciation for our work. I walk down the steps to the employee room past youngsters lying on couches and chairs watching game six of the NBA finals.

summer night
insects fluttering
around the lamps

After a lengthy journey, I step through the checkpoint where the movie is to be shown, display my ID, and walk to the French fry line. I get my huge juicy fries along with a Pepsi and walk towards the equally huge outdoor screen. Near the amusement park's waste can, I sit on the concrete and watch the movie. I glance up at the sky but cannot discern one star from another. The park has been closed for a little over one hour but there is a roar several yards away.

Midnight—
the Wicked Twister coaster
shooting at the stars

Couples lie on blankets in loving embrace. On the screen, the "Thing" clops towards his goal. I am entertained by the metamorphosis of humans into superheroes and villains.

moonlit night
a spider's web forming a net
in my hair

Frederick Ace: A Haibun

The small mouse approaches and wiggles its nose. We
linen room workers are amazed. Though the place prob-
ably has a good number of mice, I declare it as being
none other than Frederick Ace.

Two weeks ago we had seen a mouse dash from under
the huge scale and head for the door. I sought names for
our new mascot. Justin, the "playa" of the place, called
it "ace." Holly, a little hottie, named it Frederick. So, I
had settled on Frederick Ace the Mouse.

Last week, we had seen a cat stalking the place. That
afternoon Holly came to me with tears in her eyes.
"Frederick is dead." She hustled me to the spot where
crushed bones and fur shared space with the bottom
wheels of our huge linen cart. "That's not Frederick
Ace," I had said, trying to soothe her.

So today, Frederick scuttles up to me as if to say, "Here
I am." It then begins to roam around the place for a
while before one of the bosses stomps her foot and scares
it away.

heat
mouse droppings on top
of the clean linen pile

.

Welcome to Sandusky, Ohio

Photos from a Life

Gloria Stallings Gilmer, mother, with
baby Francis Wesley Alexander, 1950
Below, Francis at age one

Grandmother Marie who raised Francis, 1948

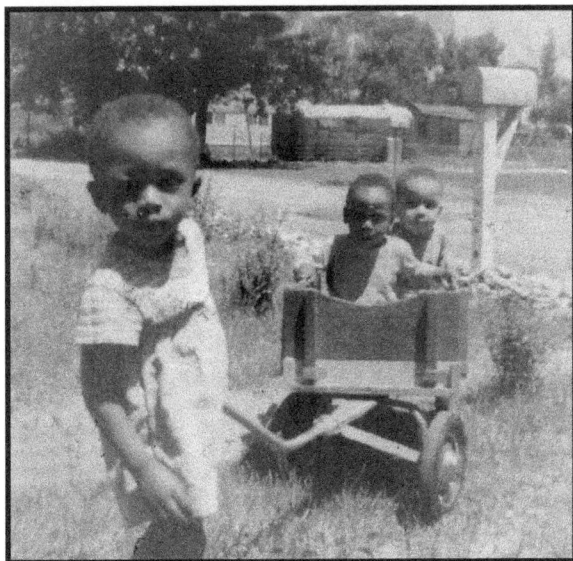

Peck Thomas, Cliff McNair, Francis 1952

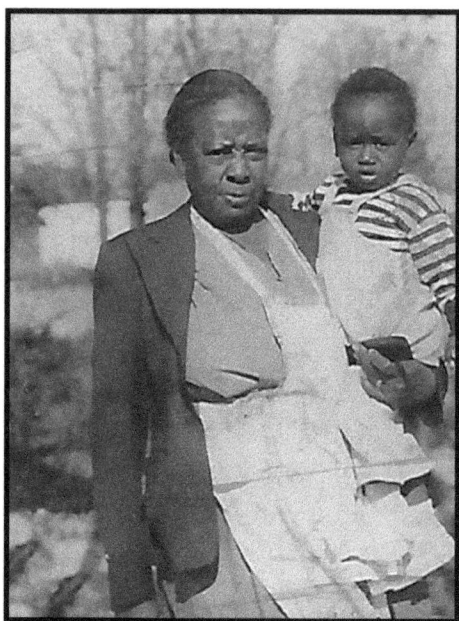

Effie McNair with Cliff McNair;
caregiver to young Francis, 1951

Grandmother Marie Alexander main
caregiver to young Francis, 1952

William (Bill) Stallings holding Francis, 1953

Lloyd Alexander (Grandfather to Francis and champion
checker player) with Theodore Alexander, 1959

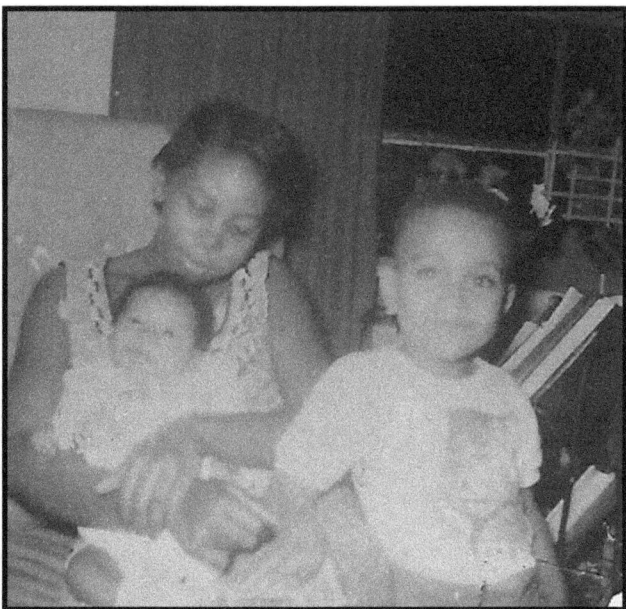

Francis with Ms. Sadie and baby Darlene
who was taken from her, 1953

Robert Rice with Gene Leighton, who
become involved in a knife fight outside of
Grandmother's house, 1951

William (Bill) Stallings, far left with
fellow sailors, 1957

Collision of *Stickleback* and *Silverstein* ship, 1956

Effie McNair, 1970

Jeff Goodsite, Linda Gruhlke, Francis, David
Nims, (unknown student) Connie Englehart
at Mills School, 1962

Nights in Blue Satin: A Haibun

I sit here at the computer and watch the Cedar Point
Cam as a truck runs down the midway. That brings
back memories of those late nights in the sixties when
this former dishwasher and busboy walked to the park-
ing lot. The sound of the packs of pigeons scavenging for
food and gulls squawking overhead stabbed the silence.
Occasionally, someone could be heard playing Cream or
Hendrix on their transistor radios. Sometimes I saw a
couple strolling arm in arm.

In the seventies when I worked as a policeman, the
sound was deadening to the ears as I made my rounds
of the Midway area. Overhead, the cables of the Skyride
swayed a bit. As in earlier times, the garbage trucks
made their rounds. Even in the eighties when I worked
as a busboy, the place sometimes looked as if it were
emboldened in blue light. Sometimes, crews could be
seen testing the Wild Mouse roller coaster. Although
the place had been given a facelift over the years, the
nineties were no different. An insomniac wouldn't have
a hard time falling asleep if they camped on the cause-
way and listened to the roar of the water on the beach
nearby.

rising temperature

a bird struts on the green asbestos roof

next door

When the twenty-first century came, I could be found
working in housing and laundry. International workers
were now as common as college students from through-
out the US were in the earlier century. It was nice
seeing the mix of employees at the Cedar Point Bash

the company gave every year. On those nights, employees rode free on the Mean Streak and Shoot the Rapids coasters. At night, only the scenery had changed. It's as if generations of birds had come to relive the experiences of their ancestors.

spring
the day's temperature teetering
from cold to hot

On the Road: Michigan Memories

Bicycle Path: A Haibun

Two girls sit on the bench outside the glass-walled bus shelter where I sit. Suddenly, one girl starts running. "Bees!" she shouts, sprints past the side of the shelter, and heads for the Farmer Jack store behind me. It looks like a gray cloud that travels level with my six foot, two inch chest—too large to be a sphere of gnats. The transparent football-shaped object is about three yards long and two feet thick. The formation has a tail that dangles two feet off the ground. Each insect can be spotted as the parade slowly passes. They travel in silence, move unfazed down the bicycle path on the side of the road.

I turn and search for the girl. She must have entered the store. When I look at the path, the bees are gone.

scorching heat
munching on a free sample
of honey baked ham

Giving: A Haibun

After a cold day of collecting cans, I headed towards the
University of Michigan's undergraduate library. Ear-
lier I had bought a four-in-one Reese's Cup with some
of my proceeds. As I moved between Rackham and the
museum, a squirrel scuttled up to within a foot of me,
its arms stretched out and tail undulating. "Here, little
fellow," I said, broke off a piece of candy, and tossed it.

our meal

a squirrel rotates and nibbles

the morsel

Still Sheltered: A Haibun

I slide the drapes and watch the flakes fall from the sky. The snow appears to be level with my window. Earlier there was a news report that many businesses, including the courthouse, were canceling service for the day. The snowstorm has given me a short reprieve. I'll call and inquire about the next landlord/tenant court date. Hopefully, my unemployment check will arrive before then.

the warm apartment

a thick layer of snow

on the mailbox

Shaken Jake: A Haibun

We see each other. He stands near the corner of State Street in Ann Arbor. Wearing a wide brim, he plucks on his brown guitar. "You on the move," Shakey Jake asks me. I respond, "I am on the move, Shakey Jake."

"Alright then." Words of philosophy flow out of his mouth.

"Chicken aint nothing but a bird. Either way you split it." He reminds me to buy one of his cassette tapes. No money, but my intention is good. He is part of the history of Ann Arbor and the inspiration of my life as I struggle to improve myself here.

The street musician plucks on his guitar and sings, adding his own words as he goes. I watch as some people throw money in his guitar case. His influence moves me, makes the legs move faster, invites the muse to follow me home.

I stayed in Ann Arbor from 1987 to 1995, left, and returned in 1999. Chest expanded, Jake showed me the huge sombrero-like hat he got from New Orleans. I last saw him that winter of 2005. He died in 2007.

a moth bumping

into the windchimes

xylophone dreams

Detroit

Captain: A Haibun

On the Greyhound heading to Detroit for Christmas, a
young soldier dressed in green fatigues and shiny black
boots chats with a boy. With his small brown hands, the
child shows the man how to use the armrest. He calls
the soldier a "Captain." On arrival, the kid says, "Bye,
Captain." The regular points to the insignia above his
name tag, says, "I'm not a captain, I'm a private." The
boy smiles and says, "Goodbye, Captain Pirate."

crowded bus station

the rat-ta-tat-tat

of a video game

Momma Gladys: A Haibun

Gladys Beard Stallings' home was a "stopping place" as I described it in the Summer 1991 issue of AIM Magazine. I'm one who stopped by and stayed in that Highland Park address, three blocks from the Reverend C.L. Franklin's home in 1973. The tall light complexioned woman was my grandfather's second wife. I had met my grandfather William and their children a year earlier when they came to Sandusky. When I went to Detroit to visit one summer, she invited me to stay and finish my schooling. That fall, I enrolled at Wayne State University.

Veteran's Home

stopping for a family of geese

to cross the road

My stay with her brought many opportunities and memories. If anyone could be called a superwoman, it was her. She juggled a life with a house of three girls and two boys, being employed as a social worker, and working on her master's degree. It's the cooking I can't forget. She has some of the best spaghetti I have ever eaten. Pleasant to the eyes like the stringy pasta, her long black silky hair flowed down to the middle of her back.

summer Detroit

the Chrysler plant

showing signs of life

Many were the weekend nights when the Beard family partied at her big yellow house with its brick porch that looked like the parapets of the Alamo. Between the professionals and family members, there was plenty of

intelligent conversation, music and dancing. Her wise
mother, affectionately known as Grandma Emma, would
be at many of those festivities. Emma would later go
on to get her high school diploma at age ninety. Gladys'
brother Arthur Beard, the second ranked Black comput-
er specialist in the world, also came to the parties.

cool breezy Summer
silence in the men's room
at Belle Isle

I remember when Gladys made news nationally. She
had rescued a kid named Lamont from his drug infested
surroundings. In 1986 her life story was published in
Life Magazine. Since that time, Gladys' son Cliff started
a computer company where they worked for the Detroit
Water Department and Detroit Public Schools. All of
her children and grandchildren worked in some capacity
in the computer or education fields. She and the family
have also run a summer camp for inner city youth. Her
daughter Donna is an Evangelist and Lathrup Village
city council member. Herself, Momma Gladys is now
retired. And although she sometimes forgets things, she
can still cook up a great batch of spaghetti.

warm Easter breeze
in the cultivated garden
a rabbit

Detroit Moments

autumn festival
the old author hugging
boxes of microfilm

        the year ends
        the elderly lady shuffles snow
        to feed the pigeons

saxophonist
weaving jazz sounds
into blue and red streams

deep cold
vacant factory buildings
and a bus stop

Detroit winter night
the alto saxophone's notes
skate along the snow

Winter night
the trombone stitches and mends
our aching ears

Outside the jazz club
yellow lights flash in rhythm
to the wiggling horn

Spring Detroit
the saxophone's cry echoes
off vacant buildings

Jazz club's spring nights
from open door, the horn's sound
wiggles through the air

cool silent breeze
inside the halfway house
ex-convicts yelling

tranquil spring day
the prisoner's snail's-pace mopping
of the unswept floor

Summer Detroit
in gasoline water puddles
pigeons mix colors

summer heat
the silent calculated move
of the chess player

Summer's eve
the sun is webbed
in silk threads

Back in the Hood Moments

little feet scurry
and beams pulse from tiny fists:
lightning bug

rain shower
wafting from the old bottle
a scent of cologne

Swirling heat
holding the toy high
the child shouts, "Circle!"

between dark clouds
a meteor's thick yellow spurt
past the lone star

the yard finally scythed
combing mint scent
from my hair

glazed ham—
a strong wind carving
the fresh coat of snow

fog
long after our goodbyes
his ghost story lingers

More on the Road Moments: Ohio

tenth floor heat
fireworks here and there
along the horizon

        the silver can
        jutting from the deep depression
        hills of snow

Gray fog
a transparent brush
amongst the trees

                              mountain cabin's railing...
                              my feet planted firmly
                              against the landscape

Early summer morn
the fog lifts sheet by sheet
off the fields

summer heat
the white line scampering
across the street

Near the atomic plant
splitting the atom
with jazz song

torrid summer eve
in the trench the beaver's back
turned to the highway

Home Again, I Reckon

Family: A Haibun

I look at my grandmother Marie's album and remember. This particular scrapbook has pictures of a lot of people named Pocock in it. I imagine she might have babysat for them. As a child, I witnessed her babysitting and being a foster mother. One baby she fostered was named Darlene. Ms. Sadie was Darlene's mother. I'll never forget that traumatic event when a social worker walked into the house and took Darlene away from her mother. Grandma cried, Darlene screamed, and Ms. Sadie wept.

winter afternoon
discovering a new cat litter
behind the curtain

Years later, many people gave her the title of The Town Babysitter. During my teenage years, the house was always rocking. Our neighbor Jill would help her feed and change the babies or watch over them. Many of the kids and babies danced and rocked in front of the console. When I was away at college, she started taking some of the kids to nearby places like African Safari Wildlife Park in Port Clinton. Some of the children affectionately called her Aunt Marie. Some of those kids became star athletes while others are professional principals with names like McDonald-Butler and Pace.

scorching heat
my telescopic gaze at
a family of stars

That Nasty War: A Haibun

I remember some of those who didn't make it home from Vietnam. Dave Levier had played fullback for our state championship Blue Streaks. Big Stew Williams, who was an earlier All American fullback for the Streaks, had a brother who was one of the first Black Sanduskians to die in the war. I will never forget our Sunday school teacher's son, Herman Gant who died as a medic in the war. There was my friend and classmate, Dent Moore, a Green Beret who never made it to the war. An automobile accident took his life. Then there are those who came back alive, like Frank.

prisoner of war

emasculated by

news from home

It was around my fifth-grade year that Frank's family moved across the street from us. He had a fine mocha complexioned sister named Annie whom I had a crazy crush for. Frank was muscular and fearless. His walk exuded confidence. Years later, the Fonz of the tv show Happy Days would remind me of Frank. To me, the short, muscular dude could wink at the juke box and make it work just as Fonzie had done. Many years after the war, I visited some friends and Frank was there. That's when I found out that Frank had been a prisoner of war.

warm breeze

a veteran tossing crumbs

to the pigeons

A Winter's Day at the Laundromat: A Haibun

After being pushed through the doors by the chilly wind, I smell the sweet scent of washing powder as I walk between the rows of laundromat washers. Standing in front of the dryers, I watch a child attempt to force an empty detergent box into the small mouth of a trashcan.

On the wall above the dryers the owners have mounted washing items from the past. A plastic washboard brings back memories of the wooden one with metallic ribs that my grandmother used. I never saw her use it, but I remember the long line that held the wet clothes and sheets flapping in the wind in my backyard.

The child continues to be a "helper" as his mother talks. She brushes his hands away from the laundry basket and gives him a bag of Doritos. I look up and spot an old box of Argo starch. When I was younger, Grandma would let me eat them. Those little bits of carbohydrate were very tasty and when she wasn't around, I'd eat almost a quarter of the box's contents in one go.

munching on chips—
the loud snap of an icicle
near the window

Ohio Veteran's Home: A Haibun

"Do you know what these are?" Uncle Billy, his askance look accented by squinting eyes, points to the insignia on his submariner's cap. It's been years since I've heard the explanation, if ever.

"They look," I say, "like fish enclosing a submarine."

"Dolphins aren't fish," he says. That's Uncle Bill, still feeling the need to teach me something. "Whenever sailors were stranded at sea," he continued, "perhaps after their ship had sunk and they clung desperately to the floating debris, the dolphins would come and nudge them towards land. You heard the expression of dog being man's best friend? Well, the dolphin is the sailor's best friend."

on the menu
in the huge mess hall
crappie and catfish

Generations: A Haibun

After moving here in March, the first thing I encoun-
tered was a group of cats. Apparently, the people down-
stairs drew them here with leftover food. Seeing the
felines brought back memories of my childhood when
cats roamed the neighborhood.

kittens at play

scat(ter) when I open the door

late summer morning

We had a black cat when I was a kid. There was no such
thing as kitty litter and many times, we searched fran-
tically for the source of that awful smell that seemed
to hover in the air. In spite of the inconvenience, my
grandmother obviously loved cats. They'd always come
to the back yard after finding a way past our fence. She
would set plates on either side of the sidewalk in the
back yard. Part of the menu was food scraps, cat food,
and pet milk. The felines came through the alley from
the Cat Lady's house. In our hood, the Cat Lady was an
old white lady who hobbled around her back yard with
cries of "Here kitty-kitty-kitty."

many moons

my widowed grandfather

still feeding cats

Now my property is vacant, the house gone. I live on the
second floor of an apartment across from my lot. I feed
the felines and let some of them stay with me. There's a
cat with a white streak running down its nose, orange
cats, a grey cat with a white dot on its back and mix

matched white and black legs, and black cats making their way up my concrete steps. Could these felines be descendants of the ones I saw those many years ago?

cool breeze
the kitten jabs, bites, then hugs
this feathery toy

Home to Stay Moments

paralyzed on her right side,
to the music Grandma moves
her left toe

Migraine Haiku Poem

sudden#rai##shower
attemp#ing##o type poems
with o#e e## open

"Crack-a-day-o!"
velvet feathered Forster's Tern's
wake-up call

pigeons displaying
a kaleidoscope of breasts
in the fountain

rainy fall morning
the slug's wet trail
scarring my blue rug

cool fall morning
the heavy plop
of the green grasshopper

fan's whir—
memories of his thunderous shouts
years after the drowning

football Saturday
steady drone of the blimp
heading for Ann Arbor

frigid fall morning
the firefly's slow trek
across my windowsill

wintry dawn
my failed garden
now an ice rink

winter twilight
patches of blue jigsawed
across the white bay

frigid night
the squeezed funnel of smoke
arching from the chimney

glazed ham—
a strong wind carving
the fresh coat of snow

near the chili-scented house
the crackling snap
of ice coated grass

spring weeding
a four leaf clover lost
in a sudden wind

April Fools Day
the escaped fly
chilled by snowflakes

Years after her death
I silently celebrate her birthday
this Mother's Day

                              hot
                              the tiny worm stuck
                              to the gardening glove

from beads of rain
the small moon's gleam
on the spider's web

a small caterpillar
on the raised stick—suddenly
spinning itself down

the rain puddle
reflecting street corner memories
the big dipper

hot breeze
small fissures branching
throughout the garden

blue winged warbler
singing z zee-e z zee-e
our summer return

Summer morning
tanker ship's smoke is chased
by the cool rain

```
green          cicada
sways from  side
     to side       to side
side            to side
```

```
                    the toddler's reach
                    for my wiggling fingers
                    gentle wind
```

scorching heat
the thick worm's plummet
from the dug up clump

under bent weeds
a small patch of strawberries
draped by spiders' webs

sparkling white streams
freely skating against the blue:
gulls above the bay

    heat
    the wasp's tick, tick, ticking
    against the light bulb

humid afternoon
the spider's thin bridge
to the tall desk chair

with each swing of blade
a fresh mint scent
fills the hot air

sunset
a dead fish floating
from crest to crest

tranquil morning
years after his death
Grandpap's tobacco scent

veteran bugler
attacks the horn
still at war within

old crumbling wall
a testament to the force
of free elements

football Friday night
the silence tells me
who's winning

The Room: A Haibun

I miss them, the wheeling-and-dealing gamblers who wagered in my bedroom on the weekends when I was a child. "Hey big head," my uncle Bishe shouted, "Go to the store and get me some chips!" I ran errands for tips during the day and spun 45s at night. The gamblers shouted their requests and I played the forty-fives—I remember Jackie Wilson's "Lonely Teardrops" and Ben E King's "Stand by Me." I can still hear the clinking sounds of the money and see the smoke hovering over their heads. Faces taut, they tossed money and chips on the table, made their bids. During all the times they gambled in my room, there was only one fight. It's said that at my grandfather's request a one-legged man named Mr.Gene and a younger knife wielding man went outside to settle their differences. Mr. Gene quickly dispatched the man with a couple thrusts of his crutch.

old poker room
Saturday nights now filled
with sounds of typing

A Village: A Haibun

Saturday morning, Billie Jean, my pregnant cat and Hanni, her daughter, seem to have disappeared. Had she, I wondered, given birth. I soon found out when I saw her followed by Hanni leaving the spot where she usually gives birth. The evidence was her stomach, which had been chock full on Friday, but was sagging that morning. I learned something about cats over the next few days as I watched her and Hanni groom each new offspring. I was more enthralled at seeing Hanni acting as midwife. It reminded me of childhood times on the Southside of Sandusky.

In the early sixties, before Grandma Marie had her day-care center, she babysat her friends' children. When Mr. and Mrs. Horn wanted to go out to see such entertainers as James Brown and Marvin Gaye at nearby venues, Grandma took care of their children: Gary, Curt, Lynn, and Debbie.

In the later years, I watched as Debbie Horn babysat the McDonald kids who lived a few doors down. Although Debbie now stays in Detroit and Sharon is an important figure in the Toledo Public School system, I can still see little Sharon and her brothers playing under Grandmother's and later Debbie's tender care.

sunrise

pregnant kitten learning to grip

her mom's newborn

Forbidden Haibun: Old School

Cool breeze at dusk: glancing at the roof of the abandoned house. Summer surfing: attracted to the Southside4Life page on Facebook. Ominous cloud: seeing the bad tidings about Mills School. Near cloudless day: the old school building looking like it was just built. Warm shade: strong appearance on the outside but crumbling within. Weed infested lot: thoughts of past neighborhood schools now gone. Scorching heat: the baseball diamond and basketball courts are history.

whistling wind

the ghostly sound

of kids at play

Glare: memories of black soldiers performing in the school auditorium. Daylily: bursting with pride for my neighborhood school. Recollections of singing "We Are Mills," our school fight song.

sunrise

the downstairs neighbor blasting

old school music

The Pre Home-Going Party: A Haibun

After they pull the plug on Mom's life support, the nurse lets us fill the room. She brings us soft drinks, water, and cookies, and suggests we huddle around the bed and tell stories because, like us, she believes comatose patients can hear. After a few amusing tales are told, my sister Charita belts out the religious song. "Lay My Burden Down."

chilly night

a patient tells the nurses

the radio's too loud

While they sing, my mind is filled with memories. Many were the times I sat in her apartment and spun 45s. She especially liked the Motown artists and James Brown. Other times, my stepfather, Big Mack, entertained her with a Temptations song, crooning, "As pretty as you are..."

As the years progressed, Charita's gospel singing reputation helped transform Mom's likes into religious music. Now she, Dameka, and Aunt Donna take turns leading. "He's my rock," one sings, while the others follow with the refrain, "I love to praise his name."

the comfort of home

listening to record

after record after record

[Note: In some Black churches, home going is synonymous with funeral. Thus, I called this event a pre home-going party.

⌘—97—⌘

Graveyard Memories: A Haibun

Here we stand amongst the gravestones, three generations of Irbys' with me telling my second cousin Jamaal stories of each person a particular grave marker represents. My uncle O has just joined us as I show my cousin the gravestone of Robert "the Rocket" Lindsay, the lightning fast track star of the nineteen-sixties whom I grew up with as a neighbor. "Many was the day," I said, "when I saw him in the backyard practicing his moves over a sawhorse. At States, he would've set a state record as he gracefully flew over the hurdles with no one close to him," I then frowned, "But an official disqualified him for stepping out of his lane. He came back and won the two-hundred-yard dash."

We older men seek the shade in attempts to evade the sun's grasp. As we walk under the trees and approach Grandma Irby's grave, Uncle O spots the tombstones of various friends. He shows us the grave of someone who boxed Golden Gloves with my father. "He was very good," he says. Then he asks me if I've heard of John Mack. After I respond in the negative, he tells us that John Mack killed not one, but two people. "Whenever John joined us in a basketball game," he said, "John always won." It amazed me that Uncle O, who over the years had impressed me as fearing no man, had his own frights.

"This is all we get for all of our life," he says as we look at Grandma Irby's grave, "a tiny plot for a lot of money."

humid afternoon
slurping warm water
out of the bottle

War Between the Services: A Haibun

"Ham!"

"Turkey!"

No, it's not Thanksgiving. As a teenager I was entertained whenever my future stepfather, Big Mack Gilmer, came to the house. Mack was an Army veteran and Uncle Billy was a Navy man.

Back in the day, sometimes the marines and sailors used to fight. All that was changed with college football: Army versus Navy, Air Force versus Army, and Navy versus Air Force. Mack and Bill carried on the tradition. Mack called Bill, "Ham", and Bill called Mack "Turkey". Sanford and Son versus George Jefferson couldn't have been as entertaining.

spring rains

the once vibrant Miller Drug Store

all boarded up

Uncle Bill was quite a character, wearing his white or navy-blue uniform with his hat cocked "ace-deuce" when he was in the service. He braved the seas as a submariner. Years later, he was the man as he drove around in his white thunderbird, many times with "Turkey" as homie.

sunset

the huge house on Clay Street

no longer standing

At the Veteran's Home, Bill rode around in his electric wheelchair with the American flag waving in back, rollin' all over the place. That's usually how we met up with him. He couldn't stand still.

Though the years have passed, the air was still electrified whenever Mack came to visit him at the Veteran's Home.

"Ham!"

Turkey was no longer on the menu.

The two regaled each other with memories of the past, both military and non military. They loved to talk about the time the young well-built Mack got smart with a big man known as "Slinky Boy" in Brown Lees Tavern. "Wait here," Slinky Boy said before leaving the place. Bill convinced Mack to leave with him in the Thunderbird. They left moments before the big man returned. He could have shot them when they drove past him. "He knew my Mom," Uncle Bill said, "so he didn't shoot."

The last time Mack and I arrived at the Veteran's Home Bill was in a near coma. When we left the place, the images of the two men were still in my mind.

"Ham!"

"Turkey!"

Granny McNair: A Haibun

A river of black flowed down her back. Sometimes, Granny McNair sported cornrows. Though short in stature, the switch she sometimes held in her hands demanded respect.

"Wecca," Granny McNair said, "would you like some cupcakes?"

She knew the answer before asking.

Most of the time, I got her cupcakes for free. Out of this world, they were like none I had ever eaten. The cake was sweet ambrosia. I ate that first, before eating the white or chocolate icing.

This memory was given to me by my friend Cliff's grandmother. Rumor had it that the woman was a Black Indian. To me, the proof was when I saw the large quilt extending from the northern to the southern wall of the McNair garage. I never knew if the lady who always said, "I reckon", had finished it, since I went away to college.

Indian summer

the moon dances between

piles of melted snow

Francis Wesley Alexander is a native of Sandusky, Ohio. He has worked in the service industry, as an adult education teacher in Detroit and Ypsilanti, a substitute teacher in Ypsilanti, Pittsburgh, and Ann Arbor, a community college instructor in Ann Arbor, laborer, a math tutor, and writer. A graduate of Sandusky High School, Wayne State University, and Eastern Michigan University, he is the author of two books of fiction. He has been published in numerous haiku, haibun, science fiction, and horror publications and in anthologies worldwide.

Wes is the author of *While Treating My Lady at Zom's Rib Shack, The Waiter Inquired How I Escaped the Pot* from Panic Press and most recently is the author of *When the Mushrooms Come* from Alban Lake Publishing.

Francis is currently an online scorer with Pearson Measurements. Besides taking care of his cats, he is an avid sports fan, amateur genealogist, and coin and stamp collector. He lives in Sandusky and is the father of one child.

Bibliography of Haiku and Haibun

"Brutally cold nigh," *Micropress New Zealand*, vol. 2, Issue 2, March 1997; "The Stickleback haibun," *Simply Haiku*, Summer 2007, vol.5, no. 2; "A Parent's Workday haibun," *Simply Haiku*, Spring 2008, vol.6, no. 1; "frigid day", *Simply Haiku*, Autumn 2008, Vol.6, No. 3; "Football Friday nigh," *Brussels Sprout,* Volume XI:1, January 1994; "spring shower," *Heron's Nest*, Volume III, Number 3, September 2006; "summer heat," *Haiku Quarterly*, Summer 1990; "receding thunderstorm," *Black Bough*, number nine, 1997; "badminton," *Frogpond* XXI:1, 1998; "Summer evening', Brussels Sprout, Volume VIII:1, January 1991; "Summer evening," *The Red Pagoda*, Vol. V, No. 2; "Hot summer nights," *The Red Pagoda*, Vol. V, No. 1;"Summer afternoon," *The Red Pagoda*, Vol. V, No. 1; "behind the dragonfly," *Haiku Headlines*, Volume 6: Number 3, Issue 63, June 1993;"summer morn," *Micropress New Zealand*, vol. 2, Issue 2, March 1997; "Blue Light haibun," *Contemporary Haibun Online*, Jan 1, 2012, vol 7 no 4; "Approach haibun", *Stylus Poetry Journal*, March 2007; "Shocks haibun," *Contemporary Haibun*, Summer 2005, vol 1 no 2 ; "Fantastic haibun," *Contemporary Haibun Online*, September 2006, Vol. 2, No. 3; "Frederick Ace haibun," *Contemporary Haibun Online*, March 2007, Vol 3, no. 1 ; "Bicycle Path Haibun," *Stylus Poetry Journal*, 2008; "Giving haibun,", Stylus Poetry Journal, 2002; "Still Sheltered haibun," *Contemporary Haibun*, Fall 2005, vol. 1, no. 3; "Captain haibun," *Stylus Poetry Journal*, March 2007; "the year ends," *Mainichi Daily News*, Saturday, Feburary 8, 1997; "saxophonist," *Modern Haiku*, Vol. XXI, No. 3, Autumn 1990; "Detroit winter night," *Japanophile*, Volume 17, Winter 1993; "Winter night," *New Cicada*, Vol. 8, no. 2, Winter 1991; "Outside the jazz club," *New Cicada*, Vol. 8, no. 2, Winter 1991; "Spring Detroit," *New Cicada*, Volume 8, Number 2, Winter 1991; "Jazz club's spring nights," *Brussels Sprout*, Volume VIII:2, May 1991; "cool silent breeze," *Piedmont Literary Review*, Volume XVII, Number III, 1994; "tranquil spring day,"*Hobo Poetry Magazine*, Issue 11, December 1996; "Summer Detroit," *Mainichi Daily*

Poetry Magazine, Issue 11, December 1996; "Summer's eve," *New Cicada*, Volume 7, No.2, Winter 1990; "little feet scurry," *The Red Pagoda*, Vol. V, No. 2; "a small caterpillar", *Modern Haiku* Vol. XXVIII, No 3, Fall 1997; "Swirling heat," *Micropress New Zealand*, vol. 3, Issue 4, May 1998; "between dark clouds," *Micropress New Zealand*, vol. 3, Issue 3, April 1998; "the yard finally scythed," *Frogpond* XXI:2, 1998; "glazed ham –," *Simply Haiku*, Spring 2008, Vol.6, No. 1 ; "fog," *Simply Haiku*, Spring 2008, Vol.6, No. 1; "tenth floor heat," *Micropress New Zealand*, Vol 5,issue 1, Jan/Feb 2000; "the silver can," *Micropress New Zealand*, vol. 2, Issue 3, March 1997; "Gray fog," *New Cicada*, Vol6. 8, no. 2, Winter 1989; "mountain cabin's railing...," *Modern Haiku*, Vol. XXII, No. 1, Winter-Spring 1991 ; "Early summer morn," *New Cicada*, Volume 8, Number 2, Winter 1991; "summer heat," *Modern Haiku*, Vol. XXIII, No. 1, Winter-Spring 1992; "Near the atomic plant," *Black Bear Review*, Issue 13, Spring/Summer 1991; "torrid summer eve," *Black Bough*, number four, 1994; "prisoner of war," *Black Bear Review*, Issue 6, Fall 1987; "A Winter's Day at the Laundromat haibun," *Contemporary Haibun Online*, January 1, 2012, vol. 7, no 4; "Ohio Veteran's Home haibun," *Contemporary Haibun*, Oct. 1, 2011, Vol 7, no. 3 ; "Generations haibun," *Contemporary Haibun Online*, April 2013, Vol 8, no. 1 ; "paralyzed on her right side," *Psychopoetica*, Vol. 33, 1995; "sudden#rai##shower," *Psychopoetica* 45; "Crack-a-day-o!" *Haiku Headlines*, Volume 6: Number 2, Issue 62, May 1993;"pigeons displaying," *Dragonfly*, Vol 15, no. 3, Summer 1989; "rainy fall morning," *New Cicada*, Volume 10, Number 2, Summer 1997; "cool fall morning," *New Cicada*, Volume 10, Number 2, Summer 1997 ; "frigid fall morning," *New Cicada*, Volume 10, Number 2, Summer 1997; "wintry dawn," *New Cicada*, Volume 10, Number 2, Summer 1997; "winter twilight," *Mainichi Daily News*, Saturday, November 16, 1996 ; "frigid night," *Piedmont Literary Review*, Vol XXIII, No. 1; "glazed ham –," *Simply Haiku*, Spring 2008, Vol.6, No. 1 ; "near the chili-scented house," *Black Bough*, number fourteen; "spring weeding," *Frogpond*, XXIII:3; "April Fools Day," *Micropress New Zealand*, vol. 3, Issue 3, April 1998; "Years after her death," *Piedmont Literary Review*, Volume XI, Number IV, 1993; "hot," *Frogpond* XXII:3; "from beads of rain," *Albatross* (Romania), Volume V, No. 1, spring-summer; No. 2 autumn-winter 1996; Volume VI, No 1, spring-summer; No. 2 autumn-winter 1997; "a small caterpillar," *Modern Haiku*, Vol XXVIII, no. 3, Fall 1997; "the rain puddle," *Piedmont Literary Review*, Vol XXII, No. 1; "hot breeze," *Piedmont Literary Review*, Volume XVII, Number III, 1994; "blue winged warbler," *Modern Haiku*, Vol. XXIII, no. 2, Summer 1992; "Summer morning," *Mainichi Daily News* (Japan), Monday, July 2, 1990; "green cicada," *Brussels Sprout*, Volume VIII:3, Sept 1991; "the toddler's reach," *Modern Haiku*, Vol. XXXIII, no. 1, Winter-Spring,2002 ;"scorching heat," *Modern Haiku*, Vol. XXV, No. 1, Winter-Spring, 1994; "Under bent weeds," *Piedmont Literary Review*, Voume XI, Number IV, 1993; "sparkling white streams," *New Cicada*, Volume 8, Number 2, Winter 1991 ; "heat," *Piedmont Literary Review*, Vol XXIII, No. 1 ; "humid afternoon," *Brussels Sprout*, Volume XI:1, January 1994; "with each swing of blade," *New Cicada*, Volume 10, Number 2, Summer 1997; "sunset," *Simply Haiku*, Autumn 2008, Vol.6, No. 3 ; "tranquil morning," *Micropress New Zealand*, vol. 3, Issue 3, April 1998; "veteran bugler," *Black Bear Review*, Issue 13, Spring/Summer 1991; "old crumbling wall," *Black Bear Review*, issue 11, 1990; "football Friday night," *A Hundred Gourds* 5:1 , December 2015; "The Room Haibun," *Contemporary Haibun Online*, March 2010, Vol 6, no. 1. "old poker room," *Brussels Sprout*, Volume IX:1; "The Pre Home-Going Party," *Haibun Today* Volume 6, No. 1, March 2012; "Graveyard Memories haibun," *Contemporary Haibun Online*, Oct 1, 2011, Vol. 7, no. 3.

www.ingramcontent.com/pod-product-compliance
Lightning Source LLC
Chambersburg PA
CBHW031142090426
42738CB00008B/1190